GRIEVING
With the Deceased

By Veronica Parks

Grieving With the Deceased

Copyright © 2025 by Veronica Parks

All rights reserved.

No part of this publication may be reproduced, stored in a retrieval system, or transmitted in any form or by any means — electronic, mechanical, photocopying, recording, or otherwise — without the prior written permission of the author, except in the case of brief quotations used in reviews, articles, or scholarly works.

This book is available in print, digital, and audio formats.

ISBN: 978-1-968682-00-2 (digital)

ISBN: 978-1-968682-01-9 (print)

ISBN: 978-1-968682-02-6 (audio)

Cover design by Veronica Parks

Publishing support by Littie Shively

Published by Channeling Evolution

First edition

Printed in USA

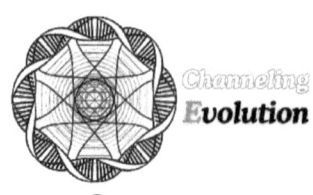

Contents

Father and I Gift to You 6

Chapter 1 Why 10

Bleeding Heart 10

Why 13

Feel It All 15

Chapter 2 Channeling With Dad 17

Connect With Dad 17

My Dad is One 21

I Love You 30

Chapter 3 Grieving 30

Last Road 31

Last Secrets 34

Emotional Wave 37

Chapter 4 Begin the Process 40

Begin Co-Creation 40

After A Dance 45

The Cry 49

Chapter 5 Hidden Memories 54

Rapid Movie 54

Connecting The Dots 57

Fun Tales… 61

Chapter 6 Fun 70

The Rain 70

Fun Living..77

Fun From Both Sides..............................83

Chapter 7 Between Living and Dead..........88

Between Worlds 88

Messages From the Dead..........................94

This is from the fellow beings 94

Riddle 104

Chapter 8 Happy or Sad........................108

Happy Or Sad.......................................108

Choose Wisely 112

What to feel?.......................................116

Chapter 9 Rebirth 121

Rebirth 121

Unstoppable..124

BE Reborn 128

Chapter 10 New Dawn 132

New Dawn 132

Mourning 136

New Day...140

Chapter 11 Resurrection 143

INheritance...143

Union with One....................................148

New You 150

Chapter 12 Rising 155

Father is Rising.......................................155
Higher Form..159
IN Light...164

Grieving With the Deceased
Father and I Gift to You

Who am I and how this book came to BE

It's a mystery for the mind to See

IN the midst of my father's passing

Channelings came to transmit through me

I came from a Family of four

Born on the other side of the World

IN an agriculture setting

Growing all we ate before

Yes, it sounds Magical now

Maybe to some of you

As a child working IN fields

Was not as exciting for me

Yet, what a true gift

For my path to BE

We grew up IN poverty

And communist oppression

Also being controlled

Veronica Parks

By the Soviet Union suppression

We came after the great depression

So much to INnerstand of the World

And I had two intelligent parents

Born with new Values to hold

My Father and I

Had an unexplained Connection

It was Beyond the mind

Or other's comprehension

You know, when you Love someone

You Feel like they truly know you

They can do no wrong

You Love them Unconditionally

That is how I Loved my Dad

There was no wrong

He could do IN my eyes

Others might have other stories

Grieving With the Deceased

And this is the true riddle of passing

Every person is someone
That we needed them to BE
The same way I share these pages
For you to truly See

You will find your answers
IN the life riddles to BE
I came from nothing seems like
Yet, I feel as Wealthy as can BE

My Father gave me Gifts
Beyond comprehension
And this book is an inheritance
Of our co-Creation

This is a Memoir for my Father
And I, as we say goodbye
We transition IN another form
To continue Evolution
May you find your own solace
IN this work to BE

Veronica Parks

Read the entire book once

Then pick a page

That calls you to See

My Heart goes out to you

May this assist you on your path

You will find even more jewels

WithIN this "Channeling Evolution"

https://channelingevolution.com/join

Chapter 1 Why
Bleeding Heart

The heart is bleeding fire

IN the agony of it all

How can something

I knew for a while

Hurt so deeply now?

My father is passing

From One form to another

And the pain and convolution

Feels like no other

A part of my Heart

Is ripped into pieces

I can't stop the bleeding

It spreads IN all that is

I step into my wholeness

"Veronica, it's part of the journey

You knew this would happen

Veronica Parks

You are a strong warrior"

Yes, I remember that
And every part of me gets strong
To BE there for my mother
IN any way I can
I have done this for so long

The moment has passed
There is me and my Father
Even IN his Spirit form
He knows how to make a joke

I place my head IN the pillow
To cry from the top of my lungs
"Dad, I only had 12 years with you
There is so much we didn't get to do"

My dad appears IN spirit form
As if puzzled by my Tears
He is like "I'm here, don't you see?
What are you crying for?"

Grieving With the Deceased

He even takes his passing as a joke

He knew how to Light up my world

The tears are flooding again

How can I stop the Nile River of pain?

I Surrender and Feel

I have done this before

I grew up with more funerals

Than weddings to fill my Soul

I was built to BE strong

I have been preparing for this

Yet, the man that was good to me

No longer appears to exist

Veronica Parks

Why

The agony of the moment
When you lose something dear
Is the serenity of Eternity
That life is real

We continue on
As the path unfolds
Having my dad in spirit form cracking jokes
Makes my path even better than before!!!

The man of few words
Yet, always great Wisdom
The rest was cracking Jokes
He wouldn't take life too seriously

He had many gifts
Talents beyond comprehension
He could fix anything
And build new creations

Grieving With the Deceased

Many loved him dearly

He had served them all

"Dad, why did life rip us apart?

Why was I sent on the other side of the world?"

I can't even BE near

To hold your hand goodbye

Yet, you are so near

You are next to me saying Hi

How do I explain that to the Heart?

The One that wants more time

"Time is relative my dear child"

Dad whispers from behind

We will always BE near

Right here IN real time

Our hearts Connect as One

Regardless of space and time

Feel It All

Feel it all until ….

There is nothing more to purge

Wash your Soul with tears

For the Glory of a new beginning

Live for those who are no longer

Live your Life for you

Live to the fullest every Present moment

May it show you the real you

You get to experience it all

The Joy and the Grief

You are still breathing and moving along

What else will this Path reveal?

Anything is possible

With your Open Heart

Life flows like a River

Through your tender heart

Grieving With the Deceased

Let's begin anew

Living life to the fullest

All we came to do

May you BE the example

Of what is possible for you

Cry a Nile River

When you say goodbye

Cry all that was and wasn't

Cry until the tears come dry

The Heart feels so heavy

Even after hours of tears

I want to rest Father

Yet, the weight keeps me up, with no ease

https://channelingevolution.com/join

Chapter 2 Channeling With Dad
Connect With Dad

Dad, you want to co-write with me
A book between two worlds to BE
What good would that do
To Channel this through?

"Oh Veronica," he said
Wait, how do you know English?
I can speak whatever language you hear
I'm not bound to One mind or language

Wait, does that mean
That if somehow, I can die
Or believe on all levels that I'm dead
What information I'm met with after that
Becomes true for me
Like you speaking English to me?

So, if on the other side

Grieving With the Deceased

I'm told that I can speak English

That becomes true

Because I Connect

To the Universal Mind, to BE?

Isn't that what life is about?

Says Dad with pride

You only know what is true about you

What you believe others telling you

Or eventually choose for yourself

So, if you are met with a being

That after your death tells you

That you could do anything you most like

That would BE great?

Yes, you call it motivation

Or inspiration,

If you receive within

And yes, it is the concept of belief

After death or near death

You receive a clean slate

Veronica Parks

To believe what you choose to

Because the past Is no longer holding you

Until then, you are being

All you have been told

And more than you choose

Alongside of the road

Okay Dad, you convinced me

Of this and many things

Now I'm intrigued

I will co-write this book

If you allow me to grieve through it

The deal is made

While I'm IN a beautiful garden

With a statue of God,

A beautiful cat by my side

Many birds surrounding me

And a hummingbird just stopped by

Grieving With the Deceased

Okay, Okay, Okay

I will take this as a sign

Let's begin this co-Creation

Between the living and the dead

This book will BE, to tell

Veronica Parks

My Dad is One

My Dad and I became one

One heart, One body, One soul

He is no longer residing

IN another Body to hold

The Grieving as we call it

Began and ended with him

What a powerful Soul

To Unite so quickly within

I asked if he would join

My writing on today's day

Because it always fills my Heart

To share this gift with those coming my way

He said, "I thought you'd never ask"

As he made his way into my field

He has been waiting for the opportunity

To BE One with me

Of course, it all makes sense

Grieving With the Deceased

This is my way of Treasure

He has become One with me

He will BE a part of my creations

My Dad continues to live through me

And I receive the Inheritance

His great humor and wisdom

Resides IN my DNA to weave with

Oh Dad, we are great together

We make quite a team

How can I not Transcend the grief

When you are showing me

The excitement to Live within

My Dad gets to Live with me

Through all of my experiences

He gets to enjoy all that he couldn't

He gets to live through me, as long as I am

Oh Dad, thank you for this Gift

You are with me forever

Veronica Parks

Before, you were bound

To a body that didn't work

Now you get to accompany me

Wherever I go and BE

I Celebrate this day with Glory

What a man my Dad was

And is, through me forever

Even at his funeral

He got me to write

And my mom to recite poetry

To set the stage for a new kind of funeral

That that side of the world hasn't seen

My Mom said "They were all crying

To the Sound of the words I wrote"

Even not being there IN body

I walked the last walk with my Dad

My presence was there

As if no time had passed along

Grieving With the Deceased

Oh Dad, remember how much I loved

Our 30-minute walks to school

I was a little girl

And my dad was a professor

It was the highlight of my day

To walk along with him

And making big steps

Because my dad was taller

And walked at fast speed

He said "You stay behind

You need to walk like a lady

With smaller steps IN straight line

With your chin up, my baby"

Those words remain imprinted

To this day IN my Heart

But did I stay behind?

Oh no, I'm daddy's girl

I learned to speed walk, with small steps

IN straight line, with my chin up

Veronica Parks

To this day

No One has passed me

IN a speed walk

And I do it like a lady,

Thank you, Daddy!

A man of few Words

Yet, such deep lessons

That Touch me to this day

My Dad was a man that brought computers

To a world that hadn't seen computers before

He was getting us ready for the future

He said "Listen you…

Another Fortune my Dad left me

Was a paper he Generated

From his first computer

After he entered all digits

Of my birth and city

Grieving With the Deceased

One line from that paper

Is worth more than any money

Can buy in this world

It was a line that kept me going

It is the light that shines my way

It is a line that allows me

To share this gift with you today

That line is ...

Are you ready?

"Come on, Veronica" you say

"Get to it, I don't have all day"

Or do we?!

How long or short this life is

Or does it live Eternally

Through every moment of Now

Okay, that line is …

Ready?

"Anything you set your Heart to

You will succeed at

And things will always
Work out for you"

And no, the papers he Created
For other members of the Family
Were stating quite the opposite
That was a paper
That I printed IN my mind and Heart
That pushed me to find a way, every day
Because things always work out right

My Father, my Father
So loved and often misunderstood
You gave me the biggest INheritance!!!!

I have everything
I could ever ask for in the world
I am

You gave me this gift Father
I Love you with the wholeness that I am
And, Yes …
We have to stock up on Dessert

Grieving With the Deceased

He said the food at his funeral was good

But it was "Lent food"

IN other words, vegan

Because people Lent before Easter

So, my Daddy came asking for a Feast

Of all his favorites….

Goodness help my Belly

To process all of these :)

When I shared with my mother

She said, it all makes sense

They kept him hungry for the last few days

He was on all kinds of medication

Well Daddy… Now

We get to eat for all those days

And all of your Favorites

It's never too late!!! Because we Continue

I Love you Dad

Veronica Parks

Thank you for writing this with me today

I wipe a few more tears….

Dessert it is!!!!

Let's live, what do you say?

I Love You

I will always Love you

IN the chambers of my Heart

I will always Feel you

Like a memory you forgot

I will always hold you

IN my loving arms

I will always share a Temple

For you to BE Divine

I will always Love you

Through all that was and is

I will watch you grow your wings

And Celebrate you from the abyss

I will always BE in Heart

And in memory of thought

I will always BE in you

The One you feel inside

https://channelingevolution.com/join

Chapter 3 Grieving

Last Road

I want to cry

I want to shout

I want to scream

The forgotten dream

Why do things end

Why do they have a beginning

Or is this just another illusion

Of the eternal life to BE

Do things come and go

For us to experience

Living IN harmony

With every being?

What if there was no end

Or a beginning

But a simple reflection

Of the moment here to BE

What if the Experience

Comes IN waves and forms

Grieving With the Deceased

For us to reflect on what matters

IN the midst of it all?

What if the now moment

Is our chance to build

As we welcome the beginning

And the end

With no attachment to things

Easier said than done

When the Heart holds things so dearly

How can you detach from the Feeling

That someone no longer exists

The tears fill up the river

Until they turn into flowers and trees

That shows us that nothing ever ends

That One form turns into another

And life continues…

to Dad:

My dad wants a fruit tree

To BE planted by his side

Veronica Parks

A fruit tree that will nourish Souls

For many years to come

You shall have your wish

That even after your passing

You still want to share your gift

That will continue life's unfolding

Last Secrets

The secrets are no longer secrets

When the veil ceases to exist

IN the middle of the last battle

All come together to finish this

IN the midst of a storm

Your brothers and sisters

Will BE called to join

To Unite IN history

No matter what the storm is

When our hearts Unite

All becomes possible

To begin a new life

The courage will Awaken

For all realms to Unite

To bring IN harmony

The last battle of life

The last breath feels so sweet

Veronica Parks

The weight of the world becomes Light

They all come to Celebrate your end

And Remember you IN Heart

Then comes the Transition

One form turns into another

And we get to live on

The body becomes ashes

And then turns into plants for all

The Soul lives eternally

As it leaves the body

To resume its form

IN a realm that it's ready for

The life continues on

Even on the other levels

Every time we mention their name

The person lives forever

They might even Continue

Throughout the legacy they built

Grieving With the Deceased

Through all of their Creations

And the difference they made

Veronica Parks

Emotional Wave

One moment you Smile

The next you feel the pain

Like a wave of the ocean

It takes you IN its embrace

The tears flood again

It takes you to another Portal

Another sweet Memory together

Why is this all coming to me now?

I try to forget

Maybe even ignore the feeling

Yes, good luck with that

The Heart is already aching

The memories keep popping

Even songs that we had before

How can all add up to now

To reflect upon?

The tears are flooding my Eyes

Grieving With the Deceased

I can't even See clearly
It's like a wave of pain is pouring
Through my body to Feel it

It feels unbearable
I find myself on the floor
Crying from the top of my lungs
Please turn back time, I need more!

Have I learned it all?
Have I received the message?
Is all that we signed up to do
Completed with discretion?

The tears are slowing down
A moment of peace before the cry
It feels that the tears are no longer
Like it's a drought of life force
So empty….

Deep breath IN
I take with Courage

Veronica Parks

I am Living on

For those who are no longer

Walking the Path alongside anymore

The zero point is here

Nothing feels to matter anymore

How can One BEing mean so much?

How can I Resurrect the part of me

That is no longer here?

I sigh and stay with this moment

I am here now

It will BE a second or Eternity

I feel it all as One

https://channelingevolution.com/join

Chapter 4 Begin the Process
Begin Co-Creation

The fuss of new Creation

Dad, are you ready for this?

All I have is time my dear

We live IN Eternity

Of course

The humor doesn't pass with death

This is going to BE

An interesting co-Creation

Are you ready Veronica?

Yes, I am, Daddy

The neighbor dog just barked

He felt my dad's presence

The cat didn't even move

He is like, I'm here for this session

Ok, everyone is IN place

Veronica Parks

Let's begin this co-Creation

What message do you have for me, Dad

What is your inspiration?

Oh, what Fun we can have,

Let's begin with religion

I didn't get that whole church thing

But now I get it, my dear Veronica

What do you mean Dad?

What about religion

Do you not believe in God?

No, it's not that

It is the Bible dear

There were so many missing parts

I didn't understand

Why the church isn't fun

Why this whole fuss

About being serious and suffering

It doesn't take much to BE Happy

Grieving With the Deceased

But this whole church thing

The way I was taught

Had nothing but fear to induce

That we should fear our God

So, we're all believed to BE sinners

And paid our visits to church

To forgive our sins

Placing the whole weight on a priest

But he was a man like me

Why do we put all our sins

On One single man to carry

Who serves God to BE

Does that feel familiar to you?

How much have you carried

The pain for those around you?

Life IN general my dear

We shouldn't fear God or death

Veronica Parks

We need to Celebrate it all

While we are here

It is part of circulation, Dear

So, what about church

Did you like any celebrations?

I liked the meals that came after

I didn't care much about the system

Don't tell that to your mother

She wanted me to believe

I get it Dad

It didn't feel right to me either

Especially with the fear of God

I have a different INnerstanding

Okay, One more thing I want to share

What Dad, what is it?

This whole tradition

To Celebrate the dead

Ask the deceased what they want

Grieving With the Deceased

Don't follow a blind tradition

Like people do with everything else

I wanted people

To Celebrate my departure

Okay Dad, I INnerstand

Should I place

The computer down

And go Dance?

Yes, my Child

You are learning fast

Veronica Parks

After A Dance

I danced my Heart out

To a song I grew up with

By George Zamfir

"The Sound of Silence"

I loved that song

The flute touches my Soul

Like a sweet sound of a world

We Desire to live on

Oh, what a melody

To unlock the Soul

Every Breath counts

The right intensity and passion

No time is spared

Every moment is Eternity

Pouring through the Sound

Of the loving Home embrace

Oh, Daddy, I miss you

Grieving With the Deceased

This song reminds me of that time

That we hoped for

We wished for a better life

Well Daddy, that future is now

I have all your favorite food

Your glass of wine

You know, I haven't had a glass in so long

I remember you used to make

The best Cabernet I've had

Your wine was truly

The best in the whole World

I have your food, your wine

A beautiful song from our land

What do we Channel now

Or do we Celebrate?

Oh, my dear Child

You picked that from your Mother

Veronica Parks

Needing to know ahead

More than you already know

Have mercy on your Soul

Okay Daddy, I'll slow down

But there is so much to live for

There is so much to explore

Even you said that before

Yes, I did, and I also promised

That you will have space to Grieve

You brought all my favorite things

But where are yours, my Dear?

Oh Daddy…

You are so good at this

You have mastered a Master

I see that your Spirit

Gave you access to your Wings

I hear you Father

I am here allowing this moment

To BE all it wants to BE

Grieving With the Deceased

We have an Eternity

Why rush this precious moment

I will play my music now

You better enjoy it

And I will dance my Heart out

Yes, but first cry, if you have to

Okay Daddy…

Veronica Parks

The Cry

Cry with crocodile tears
My dad used to call them
My big eyes will have them pouring
Filling the well from the pain within

The cry is Holy water
To nourish my Soul to Feel
It is the grief of no longer being
As I was, or believed mySelf to BE

When a BEing is leaving
Your life the way it was
It becomes history
For you to cry the tears

Many don't Feel at ease
To See another cry
Yet, it is so necessary
For the tears to come dry
Cry dear child, says my father

Grieving With the Deceased

Liberate your Heart from pain
You are crying the part of you
That is no longer Present today

Cry all that we have been through
It takes a strong person to do that
Cry the liberation from what was
Embracing your graduation day

Your tears are Holy water
The nourishment your Soul needs
Cry to wash off the dust
Of all that no longer exists

Cry your tears dry
Liberate yourself from weight
Cry from the top of your lungs
So you can BE Happy again

Thank you, father, for holding me
Your embrace truly helps me with this

Veronica Parks

Thank you for holding the space

To wash off what no longer exists

Cry and liberate yourself my child

Cry until the smile comes through

Even Earth Mother is crying

The rain has been pouring the whole week

Earth Mother is crying with you

She is cleansing alongside you

You are crying for the Heart

To continue Loving through

Cry, my child, the tears of the past

Until there is no more to wash off

The Sun will come to greet you

When you have transcended the pain

Cry, my child, and Alchemize

This Pain for the entire family

You have done this for so long

Grieving With the Deceased

Carrying the weight of the Journey

Cry that life has dealt us
A tough hand to play this game
Cry that we are transcending
To Connect with each other this way

Cry so we can celebrate
Our Union coming to BE
Share this message with the world
I will be your Archangel to See

Cry the weight of the past
Free yourself from that life
So we can walk along the path
Connecting with the other side

When you have no more tears left
And are ready to begin the process
I will BE here by your side
Whispering messages from beyond

https://channelingevolution.com/join

Chapter 5 Hidden Memories
Rapid Movie

At the end of a journey

You experience at rapid speed

All of the past memories

All that was and wasn't

You begin the flood of tears

With feelings that take over

What if, what if, what if

But now it's over…

You see the entire journey's movie

IN rapid speed and even stop

At some memories that served a purpose

What if they have already done their part?

Oh, a sigh with Relief, they are free

Free from the weight of this life

Along with the entire Ancestry

And all the others we picked up

What a journey of remembrance

Veronica Parks

You want to relive it all

So you don't miss a frame

To absorb all shared before

The journey has ended

You have completed your part

Now integrate the lessons

And receive the gifts

They worked a lifetime to build

Gifts come IN many forms

Depending on our soul journey

Could BE material gifts for a young Soul

Or it could be pure Magic

For One that came

To end this journey for good

What a gift they were in my life

What a gift they were in your life

As you and I don't really matter

It is the energy of passing

Something that no longer exists

Grieving With the Deceased

We all share this pain

This heaviness of the moment

Until we look and See the Sun

Shining silently and waiting for us

To simply look up and remember the Light

We still See and Sense

We can still enjoy the Sunrise

What a gift I hold in my hands

I want to live it all to the fullest

Thank you for giving me the biggest gift

Veronica Parks

Connecting The Dots

Jumping from One memory to another

As if I am there IN real time

Having vivid pictures and Sensations

I stop, "What is really happening?"

What are these memories

And why do they all come now

Is it to free our field

From that entanglement

So we can truly move on?

That makes much sense

But what if One chooses

To hold on to a memory for dear life

Are they holding the Soul

Of the one passing by?

Yes, in many ways, they can't leave

When One is holding a grudge

They get haunted by the same ghosts

Grieving With the Deceased

They don't want to leave behind

But Dad, that happens
IN the life we live as well
When we don't forgive
We feel the heavy weight

Yes, you are right
My sweet clever child
You always had a way
To make sense of things

Oh Daddy, stop it
That is probably
The first complement...

I'm sorry my child
Your mom and I were tough
To raise you a strong Warrior
So you can survive in the world
I am very proud of you
Even IN the Spirit form

Veronica Parks

Thank you, Dad

You know how to lift

The little Girl in me up

You always gave me Hope

That was you, my child

You have taught us all

People started paying me money

When you ask them to pay

So things don't break again

You were only 3 years old

You were so outspoken

And then you shut down

When they hurt you

I failed to protect you

From the ill of this world

Oh, stop it, Daddy

You had such a big mission

It took me until now to INnerstand

Grieving With the Deceased

What a role you had Chosen to play

I feel that I need a break

To process all that isn't

To integrate the History

And send it to Akashic Records

We are complete here for now

Fun Tales...

Okay Dad, what do you say

You were so active right before

I came to the Computer

Oh I see, I promised some Music

Dad asked to me play

"Modern Talking" today

Okay, we are set for some fun

We are in Dancing mode

Daddy what is it?

I'm here, Veronica….

I missed the fun memories with you

There is so much I wanted to give you

But my life didn't allow me to

You were my gift, I asked from God

I begged your Mother

Grieving With the Deceased

To give me a beautiful Daughter

We had prayed for five years

Until you finally came to BE

So precious

Such a gift from Universe

I wanted to give you everything

We were set for success

And the world changed over night

We were left with nothing....

Daddy, stop this

I thought we were going have fun

I have to share this, Veronica

So I can free my Soul

Yes, of course, Daddy

I will listen to it all

But please know that you didn't know

You have done your Best

You are so good to me

And all that have met you

Veronica Parks

My dear child, I can protect you now

I will forever BE your Michael Archangel

Oh daddy, what a powerful name you had

You even fought for my name, Veronica

When mom wanted to call me Victoria

Many still confuse me for a Victoria

Until they are met with truth

Thank you for this powerful name, Daddy

I learned to live up to it

That is when I truly realized

Who I came to BE and do

You truly gifted me

With such powerful memories

Remember when you took me fishing

And through rain, we hid in water to stay warmer?

That lake no longer exists

But I have the precious memory

Or the times you would allow me

Grieving With the Deceased

To ride on your motorcycle in front

Forget the law, Daddy and I

Are going to have some fun

Just don't tell your Mother

That we Love the speed high

Oh Daddy, the little time we had Together

It has been very memorable indeed

I was doing my best to be helpful IN the garage

And you would send me to the kitchen to BE a lady

You didn't want me to learn how to fix cars

You wanted me to develop my Feminine

You taught me how to dress Classy

Leaving much Mystery to the eye

Daddy, you even helped me buy

Nail polish and make-up when I needed

Yet, you never allowed my mother to wear makeup

Oh, stop it, your mother was already so pretty

But, why did you allow me?

Veronica Parks

Why did you teach me all of these?

Because you had a different Destiny

You needed to know it all and BE ready

Oh Daddy...

Remember when I picked up the idea

From girls at school

That I was ugly

And I was so distressed and crying?

You came to me and said "They're right

Even your nose is between your eyes

It was placed on the wrong side"

And we both laughed

And that was it…

With One joke

You released all projections

You have always been My Archangel Michael

I will keep the fun memories

No… wait my child

Grieving With the Deceased

You have painted a picture of me

That makes me perfect

And I wasn't that man all the way

I need to share something on this day

Yes, Daddy, I listen

What is it?

I'm sorry for those times

When I would lose my temper

And anger would take over

Oh Daddy, stop.

Please hear me…

I'm sorry you had to see that side of me

And Love it unconditionally

You had to grow up so fast

I'm sorry my dear Veronica

"Te rog iarta-ma"

Please forgive me

I do, Dad

On One level it feels like lots of weight

Veronica Parks

But on the Soul level

That was the role you had to play

Through you

I have learned how to handle real beasts

You have prepared me

For all parts of the world

And you never directed

Yes, but you always came in front

And I would be immobilized

I could never BE mad at you

You were pure Love

And I would stop

You were taming my fire

I never learned how to…

That is why is important to share

So others can learn from you

Please listen to me my child

Anger is a wave of unconscious energy

Grieving With the Deceased

Penetrating the fields of humanity

We need to tame it

To shift into the new reality

I hear you and I receive with grace

Your truth, that will help millions

I'm proud of you Daddy

You taught me so many lessons

Thank you, child

My Soul feels free of this burden

You have always been an inspiration

You kept me Living longer

https://channelingevolution.com/join

Veronica Parks

Chapter 6 Fun
The Rain

The rain is pouring

This chapter is about fun

Exactly my child

Rain is considered an inconvenience

But do you remember your childhood?

Yes, Father

We would pray for Rain

So we can have a good Crop

And food to eat in the winter

That goes with all things

Fun is not about a perfect location

Or wherever we base our perception

The real Fun is to find it IN everything

What fun can we have now

That it is winter and raining outside?

We can get some rain drops on the face

Veronica Parks

A true Holy bath from the sky!

I can wear my favorite Christmas socks

And a robe to keep me comfy

A hot cocoa with honey and music

It does sound like a party to BE

I see what you are saying

When life gives you lemons

See how you can co-Create

A whole fruit salad to Enjoy it

We were taught to handle it

Or maybe make a lemonade

But you can see it as an ingredient

To Create a Heavenly salad to BE

Wow, such deep wisdom Daddy

A perfect analogy to grasp

The real fun of this world

Well that is how I got your mother

She was so beautiful

Grieving With the Deceased

She had every suitor you could imagine

I wasn't even rich or handsome

So how did you do it Daddy?

How did you win the Heart of my mother?

How did you get her to See you

And give you that chance

When she was so focused

On her academics?

Oh, I have my secrets

But this One I would tell

I knew your mother was mine

The moment I laid my eyes on her

But how did you get her to notice you

When others were so courteous?

I had my charm!!!!

I was the chosen One for her

She was chosen for me

Come on Daddy

What did you do differently

I heard you were a bit of a player

Veronica Parks

When my mom was a Saint to BE

How did you get her to choose you?

Exactly for that my child

I gave her what she didn't have

I had the Courage of a lion

I had the Humor

And the Charm to wow her

I wasn't your typical vanilla, as you say it

I was a rebel for that time IN history

She was perfect in every possible way

Oh, I would get so jealous

You were?

Oh yes….

I sang her a romantic song

The same One I told you and your brother

She Loved the Romantic side of me

Even though she'd never show it to me

Your mom was a hard shell to crack

Grieving With the Deceased

But I knew how to warm her

And when you got IN her Heart

You never wanted to leave her

What did you do about the fun?

How were you competing with others?

I was fit, I was strong, I was Creating Fun

I was clever and had the wit Beyond others

What else Daddy

How did you get her

To kiss you the first time?

Oh, I was a player

But your mother melted my heart

I used all my wits

But I was so nervous

I showed her my cool side

With my moves and a fedora hat

Oh, I remember that picture

Yes daddy, my mom was pretty

Veronica Parks

You were just okay

But your personality

Had opened the door to her Heart

And you were forever IN

Yes, we had a life together

Some sweet memories

Others, bruised by history

You were there for some of it

Yes, life is all things

And the secret is to Create fun

With all that is

That is the key to a Heart

That might BE impossible to unlock

This was One of my secrets

I won your mom's Heart

And she carried me till the last day

Bless her heart

Grieving With the Deceased

Veronica Parks

Fun Living

Oh, how much Fun is to BE had

IN the world to BE

If I could live another week

With a Strong body

I would try it all to live it!

Oh Daddy

Yes, I know

You think we would remember

And we do as kids

But by the time we have grown

We forget how to live

So, my child

I want you to listen

Yes Dad, here is the strict teacher I knew

It is all coming back now

Okay let's get back to the wisdom you have

Live my Child

Grieving With the Deceased

Truly live your life

What blooms your heart Open

What Awakens the little child inside?

Oh, the time we plug in

IN society's beliefs

That life has to BE this way

Because everyone is doing it

Oh, Dad you speak my language

I am, my dear child

I never told you how proud I am

That you said "No…

I will live my life the way I choose to"

You were my Freedom

I got to live through you

But this is a deeper level

Don't plug into time like a machine

That takes your Life force away

You do routine things every day

IN fact, the system teaches you

Veronica Parks

But routine doesn't build brain pathways

It ingrains the way that already is

I loved fixing things for Fun

Because it brought a challenge to me

That I could find a solution

Even if no One else could see

I had Fun exploring and improving

All I could get my hands on

That allows for Evolution

Just find something you enjoy

So, like a hobby, you say?

It is more than that

Work is brought as duty for slaves

Creation is for the God within

So, you say that our jobs

Like yours as a teacher

Was to enslave you?

Grieving With the Deceased

Well, teaching is building
The children of tomorrow
But even the schooling system
It is very logical

We even taught you that way
We didn't allow space for Creativity
Because that didn't produce Wealth
We put you to work on what made sense

I know, that was not fun
But I found my ways
I had Fun making animals
My Holy best Friends

I adored the Rain
And the Sun rays
Even when I wanted to sleep at 5AM
We had to go to the land to pull weeds

Oh Daddy, we worked so much

Veronica Parks

My entire childhood was work

I don't remember having much fun

With the family at all…

The most comforting thing I remember

Were our family meals together

Talking about Hope

That someday things will get better

You are right my Child

And I'm sorry for that

That is why Fun is important

IN fact, it is why your mom

Fell in Love with me IN the first place

But we followed what was expected

I stopped helping your mom

With food and kids

Because it was not manly

I was looked down upon

By other patriarchal men

Grieving With the Deceased

Shamed for holding my own child

Daddy why are you telling me this?

Because Fun is important

Loving each other is the most precious thing

But we put all energy on impressing others

And caring about what other people think

We forgot to have Fun

And I want you to live to the fullest

From this moment now

Even while grieving

We can laugh and cry at the same time

But do not waste another moment

Veronica Parks
Fun From Both Sides

Daddy, I want to hear about Fun
From your side of the spectrum
Does that exist IN other dimensions
That you are travelling through

Not exactly IN words
The feelings are for human realm
That is the best part you have access to
Through emotions you Create the world

So, you really miss the Fun?
That is why you got me to write this chapter
Even when I was leading the Soul Healing Path
I was calling it fun for others!

Yes, you are ahead of time
IN so many ways
And yes, have Fun while you're there
Truly make the best of it!
So how do you feel Joy

Grieving With the Deceased

Or I guess you are not feeling

How can you tell what is good or bad

Or who to help and when to do it?

Your experience collects information

Stored in the Akashic Records

There is an order of things

And those with Open Heart

Can contribute to Evolution

You call them Chosen ones

From the records we intervene

We help those who can Listen

It is a simple balance of things

As we Evolve all species

So what happens for us

When we have fun while here?

Well, the real heart fun will open your field

To Create Heaven there

When you have fun

Your DNA expands

Veronica Parks

You reverse aging

You become One with all

But you don't mean matrix fun

The drinking and that kind of stuff

I'm speaking about fun of Heart

Not the coping mechanisms

You, in the western society

Utilize drinking for fun

Even the doctors recommend you

Two glasses of wine

But we drank to cope with pain

To help with our hard life suffering

We drank to celebrate weddings

And grieve our forgetting

Oh my goodness Daddy

I was interrupted

A woman just delivered flowers

Grieving With the Deceased

That One of my friends

Had sent me for March 8

The International Women's Day

Was that your doing

Is that why you inspired me

To share that poem on Facebook today

On International Women's Day?

I have my surprises

What can I say

Angels have helpers everywhere

Expect only the best coming your way

Go, enjoy your flowers

This is part of the fun

The worlds are more malleable

You are writing this book

With a deceased One

I was able to bring you Flowers

For International Women's Day

And your Angel friend Keith

Heard and blessed you today

Daddy, please take care of Keith

Bless him with infinite Miracles

He has been supportive of me

IN so many ways

Bringing smiles to me

As we Create this today

https://channelingevolution.com/join

Chapter 7 Between Living and Dead Between Worlds

Ok Daddy, you called for this chapter
And I'm already intrigued
I shall give you the stage
And listen to your Channeling

This conversation here
You hearing me
The part that I can concentrate
Sounds like the Father
You knew before to BE

You are saying that you are you,
And all that is Coming through
The personality of my Dad
All because I'm grieving?

Yes, the grieving process
Allows you to Connect this way
We are here to co-Create a path

Veronica Parks

For others to grieve

With a deceased this way

So, IN another words

Beyond the grieving part,

You are sharing things

From all that is on other side?

Yes, and almost yes

The other side

Is simply a change of form

Not another coin to focus on

The information remains

With the lineage DNA

That allows us

To Connect this way

So, because my Father passed

And I can See and Hear beyond

I can Connect to the energy continuation

After the body no longer holds its part?

Grieving With the Deceased

That is a beautiful translation
And for the simplicity of things
I will BE speaking from all that is
Honoring the grieving of the side
That appeared as your Father in the 3D

And yes, I can hear your thoughts
You can call me Daddy
Because your father is the bridge
Connecting the two worlds
Of the living and the dead

Is that why you appeared
As Archangel Michael for me
Your name was the direction
For you to find your wings?

You are learning fast
Things are much simpler
When you don't see things as death

Veronica Parks

But transferring to the next level of Evolution

I bet you didn't think that before you passed

I wasn't scared, I was ready

Your mom fought for my life many times

But I needed to serve you better from this side

So, you say there is an order

Of life and death on Earth

That the dying

Could BE called by the Soul

If they are not learning the lesson

Yes, you can present it this way

If there is no growth, no Evolution

The person will Begin to decay

Or an accident might stop the illusion

What if the person has a Purpose

But is not Aligned with the Soul?

Then you might receive many attempts

To listen and follow your path along

Grieving With the Deceased

Ok, so a part of our mission

Is to stay alive as long as we can

If we continue growing

We need to focus on

How good can it get?

Beautiful translation

You begin to comprehend

The power of every living moment

You will BE so Present with Fun

You know the way to my heart Daddy

I learned from you, to have fun

I can see how this perception

Can help with the grieving of a soul

That no longer walks this path

How can others find connection

To those that passed away?

They have to believe

And Open to Connection

Just like you and I did

Veronica Parks

The same belief seems to BE the base

Of everything IN this life riddle

All our beliefs can Create

A whole new Reality

Messages From the Dead

This is from the fellow beings
That have just passed along
Many are still lingering here
IN this space with you all

I will allow the dead
To speak for themselves
They will deliver the messages
For those guided to hear and let go

I shout to my family
I'm still trying to make things right
If they don't move along
I can't go to the other side

I speak to my wife
Sweetie, I know what you've done
The grieving is no longer
Important to the dead One
I speak to my Son

Veronica Parks

Who long forgot about me

Please think about me

At least on my birthday to BE

I am here to signal

The one that has done you wrong

No One was able to harm you

Until now, please help

So I can go to the other side

The answers will come into your dreams

We clear the channel…

I speak for my brother

Who loved me so much

Can you move on with your life

And do what you Love

So, I can come back as a flower

To my dad that is grieving me

I was never meant to stay

The accident is not your fault

I had planned it that way

Grieving With the Deceased

Mother don't blame yourself
That I was never born
All has to BE Aligned
For me to come Home

My Love please Open again
For another to walk with you
I made space for you
To BE happy with you

To my boss, f… you
Why are you still lying to people?
There are many of you
Clear your consciousness
So I can go home
And you will sleep well

To the One who stole
I can't take it to the grave
But I can stay Here

And help you live in misery

"There are many, Child

Can you go longer?"

"Yes, continue

I will write as it flows"

To the sister, my dear

You were always enough

I can't go until you see

How beautiful you are

To my Mother, thank you

You Raised me a good man

I trusted the wrong people

And now they have to pay

To the neighbor, so nosey

That stole my wife from home

I entangled your entire family

So you know what is loss

Grieving With the Deceased

Ok, let's stop here

Some seem to BE helping

Others want revenge

Does this stop with death?

No, dear

So what is to BE done?

They simply want to be heard

Or to make things right.

And what is my purpose in this?

The messages you are able to share

Will help those IN need

The messages are clear,

They have unfinished business

So the role of forgiveness

Comes IN to play

For both worlds to move along

Where they belong?

Veronica Parks

Yes, they are many

And they will haunt the dreams

Some will get louder

As the collective increases abilities

There will BE a point

With no place to hide

The wrongs must be made right

For both sides to be free and Unite

The worlds can help each other

Evolve many things

As we remind each other what we know

We contribute to Evolution to BE

So, what will happen

If people don't listen

And make things right?

Eventually filled with guilt

They will perish and die

Grieving With the Deceased

And meet the opponents

That are waiting on the other side

You are saying that what we call hell

It's not just here or there

It is a continuation

Of karma entanglement?

What about those

Who commit suicide

Who can't bear another day

To live without purpose inside?

They will be in the same dimension

Lost to make things right

They took the initiative

While the Soul still had juice to fight

What about those, who did it

IN the name of honor

To preserve something of power

Are they in the same dimension?

Veronica Parks

That is a very good question

The riddle of the history you learn

There is no saving anything by suicide

You are continuing to believe in the dream

So, you say there is no Honor

To take your own Life

Regardless of the reason

The information is universal, right?

Exactly, my Child

The INformation is

For the Awakened to know

And others to follow

So they can remember too

They can claim your body

They can claim your right

But they can never steal from you

What makes you truly Divine

Grieving With the Deceased

That is why detachment
Is such a powerful thing
Don't let the passing
Keep you too long IN grief

It is a dense vibration
And the dead might come to visit
They can ask you for help
And you get to choose the riddle

This book will illuminate
The presence of the moment
The zero point of neutrality
And detachment
From anything but Holy

You are the co-Creator
And the judge of you
You Create your riddle
And the Faith for you

Hell and Heaven is here

And IN all dimensions you seek

It is the result when the judgement

Comes to assess what you did

You are always watched

You are always here

You are always known

Wake up and live my dear

Riddle

The riddle Created

Between the living and the dead

Are to hold the Glory

For the ego at hand

To hold on to something

That no longer exists

You are grieving the part of you

That no longer persists

So truly, it is your part

To become that being for you

If you miss them

Become that so you fill

The void the deceased filled

When they were around you

If you are upset

At the One that passed away

You are saying that even death

Is not enough for the ego to get paid

If you are in sorrow

That something wasn't right

That maybe if things were different

You would have lived a different life

All the "What ifs"

Are simple blocks created by the mind

To entangle you in the grieving

Of something that is no longer

It does exist, but in different form

The part that you are missing

You were always meant

To find it IN you

To complete that riddle

Whether you like it or not

The story of the deceased

Who they were in your life

IN you, already exists

Grieving With the Deceased

If you like that part, Embrace it

And know they are always IN you

If it's not to your liking

Then Alchemize that part of shadow too

This is the Evolution my child

This is a teaching lesson

Remember when your mom

Said BE anything you want

Just not a teacher

Now look at you….

Thanks, Father, for this lesson

I'm addressing you in higher form

There is so much to absorb

From this message alone

May all sides find peace

And ways to forgive each other

May all beings move along

And Love eternally each other

May we become the mirror

Of what we seek in the world

May we Celebrate the passing

Of those who no longer walk with us

https://channelingevolution.com/join

Chapter 8 Happy or Sad

Happy Or Sad

Happy or sad, what a confusion
The great memories make us smile
Then, I remember that side of you
No longer is the way I remember you

The sadness comes through
Could I rebirth from this
The side of me
That was with you?

And somehow, some way
I find the answers within
I smile again through the tears
Happy or sad, I don't know
What if grieving is all of it?

The sadness, the anger, the passion
All of it coming at full speed
Attached to a being

Veronica Parks

That no longer is

What is this?

Happy or sad shall I BE

Answer me father, what is it?

You already know, my dear child

Feel it all to the fullest, at high speed

Keep what is for you

And Alchemize the rest

You are a Master at this

Yes, but society

Has an expectation of grieving

That is up to the person to Awake

And remember they are still Living

You asked for a Celebration

Of your memory to BE

I transmitted to the family

And they still chose mostly grief

I did too, my father

I cried at the top of my lungs

Grieving With the Deceased

I felt it all

All that I have left behind

I cried until there were no more tears

No more regrets

No more debts to pay

I was happy at last to BE

And connect with you

Fully in channeling this way

I know my child, I was there

And I still am, for all of it

Don't cry what wasn't meant to BE

You have given your best, now See

Now the sadness or the anger

Or even happiness, that is over

Will surprise you with things

With parts I didn't finish

It remains for those

Who are still living

Veronica Parks

What do you mean Father

That I should BE happy or sad

That it doesn't matter at all

As long as I finish

What you have begun?

As long as I live, because I remain

As long as I learned the lesson

As long as I integrate that side of me

As long as I am here

Happy or sad?

It is all of it my dear

How you walk the path

It is for you to cheer

We can help of course

As much as you let us, Dear

Grieving With the Deceased

Choose Wisely

Happy or sad, it is up to you

Do you want to walk this path expanded

Or contracted to the denser you

It is up to your choosing

You have the mind

To co-Create with you

Happy or sad is like asking

Living or dead, it's surprising

When you're happy you expand

And Create with your full power

When you are sad you diminish

Yourself, minus the being you miss

You are not fully present

With all that exists

So happy or sad, is your choosing

The easiness of your path

Belongs to your ability

Veronica Parks

To BE Awakened for good

You say, funerals must be Happy

A Celebration of what was

And cherish the memories

Of what now is IN us already?

Your Presence in the fullest

To what you Value most

Gave you enough chances

To explore all that was before

If they were lessons, even better

It is your graduation day

Let go of all the grudges

And live with an Open Heart

Happy or sad

Is not even a question

It was rhetorical from the start

We needed to explore this riddle

Between the living and the dead

Grieving With the Deceased

You live to continue the mission

For those who are no longer here

Don't wait to live, a day longer

Because life is now and here

Many wish to have

Maybe another day on earth

A day to truly live it...

Do you think they would choose

To BE happy or sad?

Answer this question for the dead

When you put it this way

Seems almost pointless

To miss what isn't

Because we had a chance

To BE present and give it all

Oh Father, thank you for this

I shall dedicate my focus

To BE Happy for me, for you

And all those who no longer exist

May this message Ignite

A new passion for Living

To Celebrate those

That are cheering for us

From the other side, to live

And BE Happy for all

Grieving With the Deceased
What to feel?

Happy or sad

Or shall we fear the dead

So many questions arise from the collective

Many perspectives to BE had

This is a great place to unfold this riddle

Of what is right to feel and what isn't

When you refer to the dead

There has to BE a comprehension

Of the state of being and the frequency

I speak from a higher state of being

The dead as you refer

Is the transition space

From the physical body

To a higher state of being

Or get stuck between the worlds

Creating more density

That took me a second to Write

Veronica Parks

Such….no adjective information

There are some things

That words cannot describe

Yes, that is the space

Between the living and the dead

So when you're happy or sad

You get to choose how you engage

Tell me more Father, please,

I feel so many things

Is it when I'm sad

Or when I Open to this Channel

You have opened to share

Information from both sides

Let's stay on the subject

Happy or sad?

Yes, I felt such infinite moments of nothingness

But it wasn't the Zen I felt before

Grieving With the Deceased

Is it the realm between the living and the dead?

Yes, my child, and many get lost in it

When they don't forgive and move along

So even the Living can get lost

IN this Space of nothingness at all

That is a cold thought

I don't wish anyone to Feel this

I choose to do great things

And Share this message

My Child just like you

Have gone to places

Others don't dare to go

You have Known yourself

And you trusted you

To feel sadness or happiness

It is up to you

Why would you give

That power of choice

To anyone but you?

Veronica Parks

Wow, that was INfinite

Probably the biggest gold I have received

May this Open everyone to Receive this gift

For the highest good of all

I guess I have no more questions

Simply help us all

To forgive and forget

So we can BE free and happy again

What a rhetorical question

I shall not ask that again

That is my choice to make

And nothing that was or is

Or hasn't happened yet

Has the right to my happiness

That is my choice to make

Thank you, Father for this gift

May you rest IN infinite Peace

Grieving With the Deceased

Now, I can

Thank you, my child

I will always be your Archangel Michael

Call upon me

The way you remember to BE

https://channelingevolution.com/join

Chapter 9 Rebirth

Rebirth

Rebirth the beginning

Of the new side of you

What was, no longer is

Now you have all this space for new

All that was, is gone

Hopefully you cleared the home

From what no longer brings you joy

Don't keep it for me,

I am good here!

Oh, the Humor is back

I Love this version

Of my Archangel Michael

Let's play on this New day

Of my Birth

Yes, I shall fill up the void

Grieving With the Deceased

That no longer is, that little girl

With a part of me

That can adventure

With this version of you

As Archangel Michael

Yes, please, I'm ready for this!

My day One as a newBorn

So much to see, to feel, to explore

With infinite wisdom I have

Have I gone to far, father?

No, keep going, I'm loving this

You mean the version of my personality

That sounded like you speaking to me?

Yes, isn't that the riddle

Of the Oneness to BE

Are you really ready to play?

Oh, Father so much to learn

And I'm happy to BE reborn

Veronica Parks

Having a new Connection with you

That is Aligned with both of us

Between realms to BE

May this Create an opening

For all who lost another they loved

To find a new way of Connecting

With the new version IN their life

Holding on to an old version

Stops the Evolution to BE

Opening to something more

Connects the realms to BE

So we no longer feel the loss

Because we are all Here

Unstoppable

Unstoppable, unshakable
You are, when you are back from dead
But when you endure the loss
Of the One you loved so much
And can still Resurrect to Love again,
You become a God, walking this earth

When your Heart is ripped apart
Because someone is no longer
You can handle anything
You are Stronger than ever

This pain has a bigger purpose
To See how strong you are
To Love so deeply the passing
And the One IN front

Melt the walls around the Heart
You might wish for another moment
What if you could have that moment

For the rest of your life?

Is this what Rebirth is like?
To know that you can start over
And you are stronger than ever?
Yes, Child, it is safer to Love
Than has ever been before
That is the true Power you hold

Oh goodness, this is better
Than my first day on earth
I was crying so much
Wanting to go back

Oh yes, dear Child
You would cry for the whole world
And then, you would Sing it all out
And the day would get bright Again

Is this what life is about
Being a wave, then the ocean

Grieving With the Deceased

Then begin with a wave again

Until you remember

That you are the ocean?

Very well said, dear Child

BE Born the strongest you

Your Heart is Open to Love

There will never BE a loss for you

Wow, I am invincible

I'm here and will always BE

I Love even when I'm not here

Because I always am

And continue to BE

Reborn again

Into the new me

Thank you, Father

I receive this gift

To Love like no other

Veronica Parks

Other than who I am

And continue to BE

BE Reborn

Reborn BE again

To live a new life where

What was, no longer is

So the new party begins

Can you comprehend

The chance of this beginning

Having the Wisdom and resources

To Create a whole new meaning?

Don't look back, my child

Look forward and walk with me

I'm here by your side

What was, is but a shadow of me

I transcended to another version

So I can catch up with you

This way I can BE here forever

And never miss a moment with you

This life will BE different

Veronica Parks

You will never lose me again
You have been reborn
With me by your side

We get to walk this path together
You have an ally, forever
A great One, if I might mention
So, are you ready to start over?

How can I say anything but Yes
A new life with you by my side
I can Sing, and Dance, and BE
You will always be here for me

Reborn, I shall BE
And live and Love
What feels right to us
Because I am and you are
Together forever as ONE

Oh Father, embrace me forever
I will never let go

Grieving With the Deceased

The war is no longer

We are IN peace forever

I am Born a new being

Even more whole than before

The One passing has come back

To walk with me in Unity

I am Born anew

Oh, my goodness there is so much to do

There is so much to Love and BE

How long have I been asleep?

Oh, I have Awakened

From crying what was before

The rain is retracting for the Rainbow

To welcome the brightest Sunshine again

I shout let's begin anew

Shining the Heart Light through

Until Sun comes to greet me

Veronica Parks

I am Born with you as One

https://channelingevolution.com/join

Chapter 10 New Dawn

New Dawn

It's the dawn of a new day
And the rain is still pouring
With the full moon power
Is this lasting longer?

Rain is Holy water from the Mother
She always cries when her children pass
She has to Nourish a new born Child
So it can grow and remember at last

Every passing Soul
It's a new beginning and death
It is grieving that one story ends
And a new One has to begin
For all to live forever IN Unity

The dead become living
IN many forms to pass
The Soul is reincarnated

Veronica Parks

And memories are serving

As lessons for the One remaining

The body is food

For the soil to revive

And Create more food

For others to live by

To meet the dawn of a new day

All of it is Connected

Can you begin to See the new

It is a continuation

Of what was before, but new

Day after night

Night after day

Sun and rain

Water and earth

Creating Love, food for all

Nothing is personal

On the dawn of a new day

Grieving With the Deceased

You get to begin a new story

Anything you Choose to paint

Will BE the masterpeace you Create

Yes, this is your chance

To wipe any tears you might have

And come out of the cocoon

To meet the dawn of a new day

What will BE is your choosing

You can BE the Sunshine

On a rainy day

You can BE the Soul food

On a starving day

You can BE the way

When others See a wall

You can BE Abundance

When the world is afraid of all

You get to BE

The dawn of the new day

Veronica Parks

If you choose to …

There are no limits

To a new dawn

Of a powerful

New beginning

Because you are

Grieving With the Deceased

Mourning

The dawn of a new day
Invites you to Smile
What can BE more wonderful
Than a breath of life, to shower

Imagine breathing IN
The last Breath of your life
Oh, it tastes so delicious
You want to make it last

Yes, that is the Desire
Invited to Awaken in your Heart
There is no time for "mourning"
When you still have breath inside

Every breath could BE utmost delicious
And the most exhilarating thing
If you learn to appreciate
The dawn at your feet
Wow, what an INspiration

Veronica Parks

Father, you have such a way

Of making me See the Treasure

IN all I have each day

As I write this and Smile

The Sun came out outside

I no Longer want to mourn

Can we stop that at dawn?

We say good morning every day

What are we truly "morning"

Or should we focus

On Celebrating instead

The Light of a new day?

Invite others to greet

Each other with a sunny day

Ask them to stop the "morning"

So the dead can go on their way

BE the Sun of a new dawn

BE the Light in a dark night

Grieving With the Deceased

BE Connected to all that is

So the separation can no longer persist

You Connecting with me

And writing this for others to See

Shows how abundant we can BE

When we meet in Unity

The dawn of a new day

Reminds you of the Unity

Between the night and day

Between the living and the dead

All at the dawn of a new day, here

At the moment of the Sunrise

We all cheer for you to See

We send you infinite codes of power

Just come outside to Receive

We are waving to you with Light

Penetrating through the window

Gaze at the Sun to catch us

Veronica Parks

At the dawn of a new day

This will begin a new way

Of Unity between the living

And those who passed away

At the dawn of the new day

You will meet again to BE together

New Day

You are still here, my dear Child

It is time to complete this

We can continue this conversation longer

But there is so much to Live for

If you want more my child

Ask yourself what truly is

That you left behind

And don't you want to exist

Here now?

If you are still here

Read the codes you received before

The sooner you let go of confusion

You can move your life along

I will always BE with you

I will guide you when you ask

I am here watching over

All you need is to embrace

Veronica Parks

The dawn of this new day

Staying in the grieving
Such density to hold
Can invite unwanted happenings
If that is what you're looking for

If life is what you came for
And are Awakening to this
Get up and Live your life
By loving all that is

Enjoy the breath, the flowers
The fact that you can Dance and shower
That you are Awakened to read this
And Unite together IN bliss

BE the new day
We no longer need to grieve
We can Connect to live your life
While I'm walking the path with you
The past is now behind you
Look One last time, and close the door

Grieving With the Deceased

The Present is here

Unfolding right IN front of you

Look up and you will see it

A new day is here to greet you

I'm proud of you my Child

Grieving was imperative

To truly Value the living

https://channelingevolution.com/join

Chapter 11 Resurrection
INheritance

Something new appears with Resurrection

After you grieve all that you have lost

All parts of you that are no longer

You have graduated this school

Yes, it is your graduation day

From all you had to learn

Now recap all the gifts

As they are waiting for you to unfold

The One you loved so dearly

Has an inheritance for you

The gift they had acquired

Can Activate IN you

If the One that passed

Has wronged you in some way

Once you integrated the Codes

The debts are paid and cleared for good

Receive the inheritance of the gift

Grieving With the Deceased

They brought to you IN this life
All that you Received from them
Now is igniting inside

You become that Gift
For you and those who come
To share your new Path beginning
After the end of this game

Yes, your Heart feels gentle to touch
The wounding was so near
Yet, the Soul has written this Path
That you are walking, my dear

The riddle of duality
To BE human and God
You experience the loss and pain
While living infinitely
IN a loving Heart

Resurrection comes
As you allow your God self

Veronica Parks

To Rise IN a new way

With a pair of wings

You have walked the long path

Of density IN this World

Now you have a best friend Angel

That can help you to Feel the thrill

Of being here now

Resurrection comes with gifts

As you allow the light to Rise in you

To see the beauty and the Sun

Of a new day, a new life

A new you, that gets to fill up

This new found space

With a higher version of you

Resurrecting the God

That is connected to the One

No longer with you

Resurrect my child, so I can see you

Yes father, I find the strength in all that I am

As I no longer exist as me

Grieving With the Deceased

But as One with all that is

I feel so Abundant

I feel so Infinite

I feel like starting a Life

I have written from beginning

Yes, my dear Child

You have come to See

The continuum of this life

Resurrecting your Divinity

Thank you, Father for coming

And welcoming me to BE

Of course, dear Child

You needed to See

Why did a part of me

Want to feel the pain longer?

That is the collective programing

To suffer, suffer longer

That is a dangerous place to BE

So close to the dead

Rise my child and share the Wisdom

With those who cross your Path

Resurrect from what was

To become all new

The all-United version

With the One no longer beside you

Receive the Gift

And integrate with ease

It will Unlock IN you

In times of need

Union with One

You become New to you
Once you close the Door
No longer bringing back
The version from before

Unite this new you
Embrace with who was before
IN a Light form
From the Angelic Realm

Yes, enjoy this Union
It is the best friend you ever had
More powerful and all knowing
Everything is possible for you

When you Love another
With such deep connection IN heart
Once they pass over
You receive the gift of Light
That means you loved another

Veronica Parks

To such level of unconditional Love

That they completed the Mission

IN your journey and now they're Light

IN a way, you helped them transition

Graduate from this life

To the next level of Evolution

Offering you infinity

You have received a bigger gift

For loving as a human

The One you truly miss

Is here looking IN the mirror

You became that being

That you Love so much

You helped them transition

And become who they are

Rejoice in this Union

To BE so connected to all

Grieving With the Deceased

Now that you received this Angel
To walk the Path alongside you

Resurrect as a team
With you and the One you lost
Through the Connection of this Angel
You will find a whole new family

Yes, they will assist you
Around the clock, as they don't sleep
So many rewards for you
Because you have loved so deeply

They have Opened your Heart
For you to Receive who they are
And wear that with pride
Continuing the legacy
Of the One that passed

New You

Oh, sweet Angel of Light

Veronica Parks

Here you are all new

Coming out of the cocoon

Resurrected as the Holy you

Come out to see the world

As you begin anew

Try on new clothes, new paths

This is your chance to begin all new

What would you do with this Chance

Between the two of you

You are the One living

How will you make the best of it?

Yes, with the help of your Angel friend

You get to Dream all new

A new life to begin

A new experience to BE

What will we do together

What path can Unite our energy

To Evolve our experience

And the entire planet to BE

Grieving With the Deceased

I Love this new beginning

One with all that is

Now that we are a team

We get to begin a new Bliss

What do you say, Child

How will you utilize your new path

Will you fill the space with same energy

Or Open to more than you are?

It is all your choice

I am here with you

If it is a Friend you need

I am only a Whisper away

You have a Friend forever

Wherever you go and are

So, if it's a best friend you need

I will BE there by your side

Veronica Parks

If it's a Guide that you need

Know that you already are

As I'm already IN you

Alongside you, as One

Oh, so much to Explore

So much to Experience

We can Learn how to ride a bike

And maybe swim for real

Oh, so much to live and learn

So much to Create together

Now the wisdom and power of two beings

Are paving the path with me

I Love this new beginning

Love I always choose to BE

And live for those who are no longer

I will, I am, and I will BE

Eternally here forever

Grieving With the Deceased

https://channelingevolution.com/join

Chapter 12 Rising
Father is Rising

My father is Rising

From the form he was before

He is rising higher

To say goodbye to all

Father, I remember

You IN physical form

The part of you that was so funny

And took life with ease to hold

My Father is Rising

Another dimension to embrace

His body is no longer

The way I remember before

My Father is Rising

To his new Angel form

Every being has a form

To transcend after this realm

My Father is Rising

Grieving With the Deceased

As an archangel to meet

My Archangel Michael

To protect my sweet dreams

I will begin to let go

Of my father IN physical form

And meet him again

IN an Angelic form

This part is imperative

For the Soul to Ascend at last

To forgive and forget

All that wasn't meant to last

My father's journey here

Has ended IN this form

All that he has gifted me

Is becoming me for all

Meeting him IN a new form

To continue the journey

Veronica Parks

Allows him to Ascend
And always BE here

I begin to See and Connect
With my father in angelic form
I can always call upon him
To join me IN every way
He is no longer bound to space

Or to time we hold so dear
He is no longer held IN a body
Or a collective mind of fear

He is liberated from this journey
And it is up to me and us
To allow his transition as an Angel
No longer holding on to his physical form

I begin to Open my field
And Connect with my father this way
Beginning new stories in the present

Grieving With the Deceased

With him IN angelic form

I no longer Feel the need
To look back to what it was
Storing the memory in the Akashic Library
And creating a new path in the present form

Father, as my Angel
I can bring you with me
I can reach out and have you
Always here beside me

IN this form there are no limits
To the Connection we continue to have
IN this form I walk forever
The path of Presence to BE

Veronica Parks

Higher Form

Father comes to BE

A great ally to See

My father lives forever

And watches over me

What else can I ask for

This brought the biggest gift

My father is paving the way

For me to succeed

I let go of what was

Embracing fully the present moment

I can truly See the gift

That this transition is Holy

Father how can I thank you

For imprinting the seed of life

For us to walk this path

Of soul's Ascension side

Yes, the riddle of the reality

Grieving With the Deceased

As we are accustomed to See
Transforms before my eyes
To receive all that you are to me

Father I'm so grateful
That you asked for me to BE
I am grateful for the protection
You have Ascended to give to me

I Love that your Presence
Is living fully through me
Through these channelings
My life has transformed, to BE

The gift of your Presence
To all I hold dear
You are deep IN my Heart
Watching over with no fear

Father, thank you for awakening
This side of me I hold

Veronica Parks

Thank you for the representation
That life never truly ends

I will walk with you forever
IN my dreams and awakened state
I can access the wholeness
Through the wings you now possess

Father, I feel lighter
Than I have ever been before
Your passing brought a liberation
To the density I held for so long

Father, thank you for your life
It was lived with purpose to be
Fathering me forever
Into whom I was born to BE

Father thank you for the gift
Of this Eternal life
Thank you for Loving me

Grieving With the Deceased

With all that ever was inside

Father, the gift of your presence
Makes me Feel invincible at last
Knowing that nothing ends
That everything is here now

Thank you, Father, for the realization
That I have always been with you
Lifetime after lifetime
We came to process our DNA through

I embrace this new gift
And knowing that you are always here
Gives me a pair of wings
To travel with you everywhere

This road is never ending
It continues to BE
An unfolding of present moments
For us to enjoy with bliss

Holding on to any form

Veronica Parks

Simply stagnates the Evolution

I shall embrace the ever changing

Forms of this transition

IN Light

The Light shines through
Your Heart with infinite Love
Your wings are embracing me whole
I am guided and protected by all

My Love for you has opened
A new way to See the world
Accepting your transition
Gifted me with vision to hold

I see the world so clearly
I see the fluidity of life
I see what is truly important
While we are still here alive

Father, you have brought me
A diamond Heart to hold
A pair of wings to warm me
An angelic Light to embrace
With you I have a whole army

Veronica Parks

Of angels that you command

To walk the path of Ascension

And create a whole new way

Your transition to infinite Light

Shows me where I come from

That form is a temporary embodiment

Of the light we are meant to hold

You gave me Light to See

The eternal movement of things

That holding on to anything

Stagnates our Evolution to BE

Your Light penetrates with ease

Into all areas of my life

The vision of this realm

Came to BE a whole new life

You had come to BE

Forever shifting darkness

Grieving With the Deceased

Into the Light of your wings

I see clearly, my Father

How lucky I am

To have you in Light form

How happy I am

To See you IN me as whole

I love you my Light father

I love that you illuminate my path

The Portal of this road is Open

You are showing me the way to fly

I Love you eternally Father

What a big role you came to play

It took your whole life

For me to INnerstand the way

Thank you, Father, for your part

IN this ever-evolving Creation

I walk with you every day

Veronica Parks

With small steps, IN straight line

With my chin up to see your Ascension

I will walk with you until the end

Of my physical form in this realm

I will Unite with you IN Light

When my journey here comes to an end

I will join you IN Light

When the time comes near

Until then, I will travel with you

IN my dreams to hold near

I Love you my dear Father

And I will always BE

Your desired daughter

You brought in this world to be

I Love you, Father, eternally

Now being in a Light form

I can see your Halo

Shining your genius within

Grieving With the Deceased

Thank you for this gift

Thank you for giving me this book

Now I cry tears of joy

That you had planned this all along

Thank you, Father, for being

All that I now INnerstand

Thank you for being my Archangel

With you, I continue to live

https://channelingevolution.com/join

www.ingramcontent.com/pod-product-compliance
Lightning Source LLC
Chambersburg PA
CBHW071430160426
43195CB00013B/1863